THE VOICE OF THE FORGOTTEN
AN
ADVOCACY MAGAZINE

EDITOR/OWNER/INTERVIEWER
M. HOLMES

THE VOICE OF THE FORGOTTEN MAGAZINE
ISSUE 1
PUBLICATION DATE 05-03-16
EDITOR/INTERVIEWER: M. Holmes, Voice Of The Forgotten Magazine
ASSOCIATE EDITOR M. Hubbard

The Voice Of The Forgotten
ISSUE 1
Editor/ Owner/ Interviewer: M. Holmes
Associate Editor M. Hubbard
Publication Date: May 3,2016
Release Date: December May 3, 2016

The Voice Of The Forgotten is an advocacy magazine that centers on populations that are forgotten either unintentionally but more than likely intentionally so as the subject of it is too touchy for one reason or another for some people.

The stories in the magazine will center around the stories of people who have been deemed "bad" or "useless" or even more negative terms by many in our society, government and justice system. Each issue centers on a different population as mentioned above and are factual but names have been changed to protect the innocent, the victims and their families. The authors use pen names for this very reason but please be assured each story is based on researched fact. Some of the stories are hard to take but must be told so that we wake up to what is going on in our state, our nation, and one called a nation of prosperity.

The magazine will center on a specific issue in each issue that will come out every three months.

These populations or people are:
Persons diagnosed with developmental disabilities residing in institutions, nursing homes, and group homes and in their own homes.
Inmates in Oklahoma Prison In particular Private Prisons
The elderly in and out of the home who suffer neglect and abuse
The homeless Of Oklahoma

At the end of each magazine you will resources for friends, families and concerned citizens where they can help or learn more.

INMATES IN OKLAHOMA PRISONS

You are sentenced to jail or prison for a crime you have committed or may not have committed. As sad as it is, there are innocent men and women in our Oklahoma jails and prisons due to many reasons. Some of these include but are not limited to poor legal representation and pre-conceived notion of jury because of color, religion or socio- economic standing.

Once you are there, if you have no family or friends, you soon become one of the forgotten but this magazine will tell your story. We will reveal some truths that may not be well received by the general population and for sure our politicians and those corporations that own private prisons in our state.

In the following pages, you will read several stories all based on real people and real places. The names have been changed to protect any retribution they may occur from the stories.

Story One: Murder Behind The Walls Of OSP And Its Cover Up

Story Two: Oklahoma Private Prisons Versus State Prison. Are Private Prisons Really A Tax Savers or Dens of Abuse and Neglect?

Story Three: Women In Prison

Story Four: A Cry For Help Not Heard- Medical Neglect of Inmates

Appendix: Resources for Friends, Family Members and Advocates of Inmates Incarcerated in Oklahoma Prisons

STORY ONE: MURDER BEHIND THE WALLS OF OSP AND ITS COVER UP

Submitted By: **A Daughter Who Grieves**

It was a regular day for John at his job at Oklahoma State Penitentiary in McAlester, Oklahoma. He was stationed to work in the infirmary that evening. There were three inmates in the infirmary that night.

As John sat at his desk, he had no idea what would occur in the next few moments.

My mother received a call that dad had suffered a heart attack and was dead. This was a complete shock to us as dad was one of the healthiest people we knew.

They said another guard had come to check on my dad, as they could not get him on the phone. The man was our neighbor and a family friend.

He said the inmates had not been cuffed to their beds as they should be if more than one inmate in infirmary. One of the inmates was known to hate all Correctional Officers but had never made overt or threatening behavior toward them.

There was no autopsy done, as there should have been. He said that there was evidence of a struggle and one of the bed sheets had been torn. OSP chose to ignore all this, because they knew it meant that my mom had a legitimate lawsuit against them. It meant that my mother had lost a husband at too young an age due to neglect and that she now must raise her children on my dad's Social Security.

OSP is responsible for my dad's murder yes murder and they let his murderer go free.

It is now many years later and yet I still harbor hard feelings for how OSP covered this up. I feel like I lost a very important part of my life due to their incompetence.

Picture Of The Walls Of OSP

STORY TWO: OKLAHOMA PRIVATE PRISONS A TAX SAVER OR A DEN OF NEGLECT, ABUSE AND A DRAIN ON TAX PAYERS DOLLARS

Contributors:
Mothers Of Inmates
Former Inmates
Former Employees of CCA and GEO Corporations
Advocacy Groups

Oklahoma private prisons are definitely not a savings to the taxpayers. Instead, they are a cost due to the issues going on behind the walls of these prisons. The taxpayers are paying for lawsuits coming from these issues. These issues encompass civil rights violations, medical neglect, excessive force and ADA violations.

This editor has not only interviewed family of inmates, but former inmates and past staff of both CCA and GEO Corporations. Also interviewed were advocacy groups for inmates.

CCA maintains several prisons in Oklahoma. Two of the facilities are located in Holdenville, Oklahoma and Cushing, Oklahoma. The Earl

Davis Correctional Center, located in Holdenville, Oklahoma has been cited by reliable sources to be one of two of the worse facilities for unjustified and excessive write-ups. By keeping inmates at Level 1 they guarantee that the inmate does "straight time", which is day for day. By serving their sentence day for day, they do not earn any "good time", which can mean early release. CCA makes almost 50 dollars a day in per diem so empty beds means no per diem or money for the stockholders.

According to an inside source at the Davis Correctional Center, many inmates should appeal the write up because if investigated, some of these write ups would be discharged. This person, whom we shall call Blake, was a correctional officer at Davis but after seeing how unfairly inmates were being treated, moved to a state facility to work.

A mother of an inmate who is still at CCA Davis Correctional Center contacted the magazine and tells this story:

"My son had reached level III but received an unwarranted write up and was taken to segregated housing or Disciplinary Unit and awaited a decision of the sanctions (this is equivalent to fines, loss of good time and visits and canteen and time in segregation) he would receive.
My son believed them when they told him it would go easier if he plead guilty but it did not. According to him, inmate number 123456 (not real number), he was given 30 days of segregation, a ten-dollar fine and loss of canteen and visits for 30 days over supposed insubordination toward staff. He was accused of cursing a guard. In reality he was cursing another inmate. The guard knew this but told the young man that they are encouraged to write up inmates if they reach a certain level and must do so often. He told my son that if he appealed he would win. He did not and thus has to go back to square one and start over with earning his level back."

This young man told his mother about another young man who had a medical disorder and had originally been at Cimarron Correctional Center in Cushing, Oklahoma but was transferred to a new facility. He was written up for menacing staff when in reality, he was in a stupor due to a seizure and had no recollection of what he did. He received a "Class X Write-Up", which is the worse write up an inmate can get. Receiving this ruins his chance of parole, which he was to see this year.

It seems that private prisons do not offer the same medical services that state operated facilities do. If transferred to a private prison, inmates who were prescribed necessary medication can see it withdrawn at a moment's notice. This statement comes from an ex-nurse at CCA and it was done to save the company money. They make excuses like they "feel it not needed, they do not give out pain medication and they do not have it on hand." Even inmates with severe pain issues due to debilitating diseases and disorders can find their medication for pain and psychiatric issues withdrawn with a moment's notice as noted earlier. **This is the same medication a state facility doctor found necessary.**

THREE EXAMPLES OF MEDICAL NEGLECT FROM CCA HOLDENVILLE AND GEO LAWTON: (CONTRIBUTORS INMATES, FAMILY AND CORRECTIONAL OFFICER NO LONGER WITH FACILITIES:
CCA: Inmate 111111complaining of stomach pains for about a week. Infirmary answer antacids and other over the counter, ineffective stomach medications. Inmate is throwing up coffee ground substances for a week and passing white stool. Inmate's mother calls and calls to only get this response from medical director Ray L.
"I do not give a damn about you or SOB son."

Inmate's mother calls warden, who assures her she will receive an apology but none comes. Inmate's mother does not care how they talk to her she says she just wanted her son seen to. It takes calling several congressmen and the Governor office to make CCA do what they are supposed to do. Inmate spends week in infirmary and it is determined to be a gall bladder issue.

CCA: Inmate 000000 is severely diabetic and is not receiving his medication on time. Inmate has a diabetic incident and during the episode, injures his hand. The is Inmate not treated and in addition, is written up

GEO: Inmate 012345's mother reports that her son is a left leg amputee and has an ill fitting prosthetic. Her son has a pressure sore on the stump and now has one on his buttocks, which is an open sore. This sore is a result of GEO not giving him a cushion for his wheel chair. Inmate's mother has tried going to the Medical Administrator and

Warden but has been given run around. She feels she is being trivialized, if not ignored. This reporter called and was told that they have the finest facility in state When I asked about issues such as medications being pulled, medications not available and the status of current doctor's medical license questionable, they hung up on me. At this time of publication, the inmate has still not seen a doctor and his mother is taking it to congressmen, news media and to the Oklahoma Department Of Corrections. On top of this, the facility is placing blame on their corporation for the delay in getting this young man a new leg but in this reporter's opinion, this does not negate the need for a wheel chair cushion, as this is the cause of this young man's pressure sores.

The mother of the inmate was told a doctor saw him but young man asked "How do you check for pressure sores when you are not asked to disrobe?" The mother of this inmate reports talking to someone at state level. Subsequently, he was seen and evidence of sores was found. It seems that he has still not gotten a cushion because they say he does not qualify for one. They say that since he has a prosthetic leg, he is ambulatory. However, since he cannot wear the leg, he is not ambulatory and again has issues with the pressure sores. This magazine will keep in contact with the mother to see what has happened to her son.

At this same prison 19-year-old Timmy has Hepatitis C. This facility does not offer Hepatitis C treatment and his father has asked he be moved to a state facility that does. His request has been turned down. Timmy's Hepatitis C is getting worse, he is experiencing more pain and if not moved, Timmy's father fears that Timmy won't live to see the age of 30.

Joe has been diagnosed with Leukemia and is house at Lawton Correctional, which is a private prison, owned and operated by GEO. Joe has been told he will not receive treatment for his Leukemia, as it is not cost effective. Joe has no family and Joe is not a violent offender and Joe does not have a life sentence but with no treatment Joe has no life. The magazine has brought his plight to the attention of a congressman in Oklahoma and the Oklahoma Disability Law Center.

BTW Oklahoma Disability Law Center reports they receive several complaints a month from families and advocates and inmates themselves house at GEO and CCA Private Prisons with Lawton and Davis being two of the worse. They receive complaints on state prisons but not at the rate they receive on private prisons; with complaints ranging from medical neglect and abuse to violation of ADA rights.

Disabled inmates at GEO Lawton, it seems, cannot access the yard for what they call recreation time, since it is not handicapped accessible and in fact, is physically dangerous to those who use wheelchairs and walkers. They are forced to watch other inmates go outside. The units have no windows so natural sun is not accessible from inside. When asked about this, they say they are trying to rectify the situation but it seems this has been the answer for the last six months. According to this reporter's research, the prison system and GEO are in violation of the rights of inmates who are disabled rights under the American With Disabilities Act. My question to the state is: "Why are inmates with physical disabilities sent to yards that are not accessible to them?" Their answer is that men are sent to Lawton for disciplinary reasons. My next question is: "You mean the state prisons cannot handle their own disciplinary issues and thus you use a private prison, which violates these rights, and charges more per day to house the inmates than the state run prisons do?" Their answer to this question was to hang up on this reporter.

Yes they are inmates at a private prison, which this reporter has come to compare to hellholes but the state is paying them a daily amount to care for these inmates (higher than what state prisons receive) and it seems they are not and thus this reporters likens it to thievery and abuse of power and medical neglect. This reporter sees a class action suit coming down the tubes against private prisons and the scuttlebutt is there is one in the works.

Inmates at private prisons are not offered drug rehabilitation as they are at state facilities even though their web site says they offer the said rehabilitation. If you call the facility as this reporter did, you will be told they discontinued the program several years back and when you ask why, you might not like the answer. This reporter got an honest response from a case manager who said it cost the company money to provide this form of rehabilitation, so although the web site and company website says they do, there is none. To this reporter, this borders on false advertising and she wonders if they are claiming rehabilitation money when no rehabilitation is done.

To illustrate this fact, it has come to the magazine's attention that there are very limited programs for inmates at private prisons versus state run facilities. These programs not only offer learning, counseling and time from their cell, they offer earned time, which is some thing private prisons do not want.

One prime example is a young man whose wife contacted the magazine. He is currently at Lawton GEO Correctional Facility. He was court ordered drug rehabilitation and cannot be considered for parole until he has completed the program. The problem with this is, there is no drug rehabilitation program at Lawton. They had one in the past but the corporation did not deem it cost effective and it was dissolved. The man was sent to Lawton for a disciplinary issue. This reporter's question is why are facilities not handling their own disciplinary issues? Why are they sending inmates to already overcrowded facility? Facilities that are so overcrowded that men who are not in trouble nor have a write up are put in segregation because there are no beds on the regular units. These men must adhere to disciplinary unit rules, this is not visits, no phone calls, no canteen and all property locked up even though they are not in there for any wrong-doing on their part.
.

His wife said he would not see parole this year, as he has not met the court guidelines for drug rehabilitation. His wife is currently fighting to get him moved to a facility that offers rehabilitation. The reporter hopes to hear she achieved this and is doing what they can to help her in this process.

This reporter once more questions why do the corporation and state web pages for these facilities say they offer rehabilitation when they do not. In this reporter's opinion, this is deceiving and very unethical.

Now lets talk food at private prisons. Yes, these are inmates and they do not need steak but neither do the need green bologna or raw chicken. According to a state employee whose agency works with different prisons, the meals that are sent down to these inmates is not only tasteless but also not healthy. Also at private prisons, meals are never at the same time and are sent down, it seems, at the kitchen staff's whim. One day, say at Lawton Correctional, breakfast is served at 4:30 or 5:30 am and lunch not till 1:00 pm and there have been times dinner is not served until 9:00 pm. Then on another days, all three meals were served by 3:00 pm and the inmates who are not lucky enough to have canteen in their cells must do with out till the next day. These are men, not little children and they need healthy, sanitary food served at reasonable times, not at whim at kitchen staff and by no means green bologna or raw chicken. This reporter has talked to inmates who have been housed at both private and state run prisons and they tell the story that meals at state prison are way better and served at routine times not in wee hours of the morning or at bedtime.

To be fair to private prisons, this reporter has received reports about food at Lexington Correctional Facility, where the smell and color of the meat is so bad that inmates get sick eating it or just toss it. The dining has been "under remodeling" for a very long time and this requires inmates to walk and get their food that is in Styrofoam containers and take back to their cell. It has been reported that by the time some of them can get back to cell, the food is cold and totally tasteless and not worth eating.

Private prisons receive more of a per diem that state facilities, yet is consistently reported their food lacks in the quality of state prisons. In state prisons, Sunday is a day the inmates look forward to while private prisons inmates, who have been housed there and even a former kitchen staff worker tells me it is the same thing and not enough to nourish a man.

Lawsuits are three times as more likely to come out of a private prison versus a state prison. Men who are denied basic rights including civil rights, ADA and medical care are very right in filing law suits. Men who have had medication removed due to cost effectiveness, and who do not see the proper medical equipment needed if they are disabled are justified in being upset. As their family and the families report, they cannot get answers from case management from private prisons like they could with state prisons.

Excessive write ups, medical neglect, poor food, ADA and Civil Rights violations seem to be a way of how it is with private prisons in Oklahoma.

Now lets talk violence and death behind the walls of private prisons. When an inmate is injured or killed at a state facility, the family is notified if injury is life threatening and worse if he is dead. In a private prison, they like to keep all this hush, hush if possible, in an effort to avoid casting the corporation in a negative light. "Don't Tell" seems to be the rule of thumb in private prisons. This is so unfair to family members as they wonder they are not receiving phone calls or letters and when they call, they get the run or are told "you'd get a call if they are dead." Private prisons are on lock down more than state prisons. Due to the violence that goes on behind the walls there it seems. This tension is due to racial issues, poor food, and lack of yard time and over crowding. Instead of isolating the issues in regard to racial tension as they should do, they seem to want to throw cultures together that do not get along. This reporter is not upholding segregation, but it is upholding the idea that you isolate those that for valid or invalid reasons, hate each other and just love to fight. Also thrusting the elderly inmates and disabled ones and the sick ones in with this population makes them automatic victims.

A solution might be to do what some state prisons are doing; having a unit for the disabled, elderly and long- term care inmates separate from those more able- bodied. Defining and isolating the factions that cannot live together cohesively and not promote segregation but promote less violence making the correctional officers and inmates not involved life safer.

It has come to the attention of this reporter that private prisons like CCA and GEO are some of the biggest contributors to some politician's campaigns in particular the Republican Party all the way up to the governor's mansion it seems. Let us be realistic, that kind of money is not given or donated without expecting perks. These perks seem to be allowing double standards of monitoring for private prisons, as they seem to not have to adhere to the stricter guidelines the state prisons are mandated to follow.

Private prisons are not a savings to taxpayers as shown by this article. They charge higher per diem to the state, have higher numbers of lawsuits and many are won, thus costing more to the taxpayer. Who do you think in the long run must pay for these lawsuit settlement? The taxpayers will be by seeing an increase in taxes.

It is the opinion of the reporter that private prisons need to leave Oklahoma and maintaining them go back to the hands of the state. It is this reporter's opinion that conditions for front line staff and inmates would see a definite improvement then. This seems to be the consensus of many based on the petition that is being drafted or has been by this, It is time to take to the Governor office to have them banned from state as well as the developing class action suit.

STORY THREE: WOMEN IN OKLAHOMA PRISONS

The following story is based on a true incident but due to the trauma and actions that followed the story events are changed, as are names. The name of the prison will not be used to protect the victims in this story.

Being a woman in Oklahoma Prisons holds some issues male inmates may not see. It also needs to be noted that **Oklahoma ranks number #1 for number of incarcerated women in the nation.**

As stated above, being a woman inmate in Oklahoma prisons or any prison contains issues that men may not see. The magazine is not saying that men do not see the issues and rape and abuse that women see but not at the numbers women see.

The following as stated is a true story submitted by several young women who have spent time in Oklahoma prisons for crimes ranging from theft, drugs and murder. A crime they committed and were sentence to time for, but this time should not carry the risk of abuse including rape. Read this story but do not judge the women as they have been judged and sentenced already.

Story Of Annie

"My name is Annie I was 18 years old and in love with a bad boy. "Why?" you might ask. Well today, I would tell you of out of stupidity. He used me and then when I needed him, he was not there to support me, and in fact he turned on me to help himself.

I knew he smoked weed that did not bother me so much but I never knew till I was totally involved with him that he was into selling heavy duty drugs like meth and over the counter pain medication. He told me that he would never do a deal with me there and I believed him. After all I really believed he loved me too.

It was a hot day in July and I was asleep in the back room of my boyfriend's apartment. He came to wake me up to tell he needed me to give a package to a guy when he came. I told him I was not really cool with that and that was when I saw a side of him that scared me. The look on his face scared me but his words hurt even more. He said, "Look here whore you will do as I say or I will dump your ass. I took you in when no one else wanted you and all I ask of you is one thing."

Then like a lightning bolt his mood changed. He began kissing me and telling me he was sorry he did not mean a word he said and if I would do this one thing for him he would never ask me to do it again. I told him yes but I was scared - scared of him and the drugs. He left to go meet his supplier and I waited in the apartment for the man who was to pick up the package. Soon a knock came and I opened the door.

The guy said that he was there to see my boyfriend and I told him he was gone. He said he was there to pick up a package and he seemed pissed that my boyfriend was not there to give it to him.

I told him I had it and went to the table and got it for him. He then handed me a wad of money. I took the money and stuffed it in my pocket. Next thing I know I am taken to the floor and handcuffed. Then the man is reading me my rights and telling me I am under arrest for the distribution and sales of meth.

I remember I cried and told him I had no idea what was in the package I was just doing what my boyfriend asked me to do. He basically did not care and I knew that as I knew what was in the package I had broke the law.

I was taken to the local county jail and my bail was set. Johnny was my boyfriend and reason I was here. I had this silly dream that he would show up, bail me out and clear my name but of course he never showed.

I got a public defender and he urged me to give up "Johnny" but what could I tell them? Now I knew everything about him was a lie. I knew that his real name was not Johnny Jamison. The one time I tried to pull him up on the Internet, I found that no such person with any kind of record ever existed. I never questioned him about it. I had such a crummy life I just figured I was lucky to find a man who loved me and would take care of me.

I was sentenced to five years in prison. Yes, I was stupid but here I was and here I would be. They told me to behave and with good time I could be out in two and half years.

The noise, the women some kind and some mean. I was scared as they put me in a cell that I could possibly spend my next five years in and so I cried.

My cellmate was an older woman, well older to me I was 18; she looked to be in her thirties. She was kind and took pity on me. She was there she said because she had robbed a store. She went on to tell me she robbed the store to get food for her kids but right or wrong she had a gun yes it was a toy but it looked real and so was convicted of armed robbery. Now her kids were with her mom and she was sentenced to ten years. She was now in to her third year.

I asked her about good time and she laughed she said unless I stayed in my cell and never left except for yard, meals and sick call I had no chance.

About this time a guard came up to the cell.

I recall he said some thing like "so this is the new one". The way he said he made my skin crawl and the way he looked me up and down scared me.

As he walked away my cellmate put her fingers to her lips and waited till he was way down the walkway to speak.

"Never ever get caught with him alone ever," she whispered.

"But he is a Correctional Officer, "I began but she put her hand up.

"But he is a man and a bad one. He uses his uniform to get what he wants and he caught me alone one time and made me do things I won't talk about to anyone."

I asked her why she did not report him and she basically said: "Your word as an inmate against a long time decorated officer goes nowhere. After all, who they going to believe?"

I listened to her and never went anywhere without her or another girl who told me the same story as my cellmate. He had gotten her alone too. So meals and showers and yard we watched each other backs or they watched mine.

About a month of being there, I found myself working in the kitchen. I was told that this was unusual for a newbie but since I never caused a problem, they put me there. I did not question my good luck as working in the kitchen meant I could take stuff back to the cell for my cellmate and me.

One day I was finishing scrubbing the counter tops and had just wrapped up some leftover cake when the guard who was watching me got a call on his radio. He told me he would be out in the hall and to behave.

A sound from the door made me turn my head and my heart seem to stop for a minute. It was he, the guard I was warned about.

"You sure are a hard person to get alone", he said as he moved closer to me.

I remember backing up till I was pushing into the stove.
I stammered that the other guard was out in the hall. The man just laughed and told me as his superior, he sent him on his way.

I told him I would scream and he to go ahead because no one would hear me. I struggled he slapped me and then he raped me. After it was over, he told me to get dressed and if I said anything, he would make my life hell and added that no one was going to believe a drug dealer.

I endured his unwanted advances for three weeks then one day, another young girl came to the prison. She was 18 like me but I could tell she was mentally delayed. I saw how he looked at her and knew she would be his next victim and I got hot inside.

I could not let this happen to her. My cell mate said to stay out of it as it meant he would leave me alone but she really hated the idea this girl would be his next victim as much as I did. I began talking to others and soon found there were six women on my cellblock all under the age of 35 that he had abused, some of them with children on the outside world. This young girl pulled at their heartstrings.

We made it a pact to protect this girl as best we could. We found a way for one of us to be with her 24/7.

The guard figured out what we were doing and ordered us to stop or be written up. I had enough and did not care if he wrote me up.

We protected this girl and he was never given the chance to do anything like he did to us.

One day he was gone and we were told he was transferred to a men's prison. We didn't care why this happened; we just knew that he was gone. There were issues with other guards but not to the extent we experienced with this man."

Annie is out now having served her time and given early release. She plans to stay drug free and is working at a local domestic violence shelter. This way she can help others like her.

STORY TWO

DOUBLE EDGE SWORD
CONTRIBUTED BY M.A.T.H.

"You are married to a man who is abusive and domineering and controlling. You are shut away from your own family hundred of miles away and you are scared and lonely and desperate.

He steals and deals drugs, things you do not believe in or participate in. He tells you to keep quiet if you want food for your child.

He abuses you sexually, physically, mentally and emotionally but back in the 80's, you did not report it or him. You wanted to stay true to your vows and beside; many rural police did not want to get involved in family issues. Your husband having sex with you was not rape. It was what you were expected to submit to, even though you do not want to do this.

What do you do? You endure so that your child had food.

One day, my husband came to me to tell a guy would be picking up a bag of pot and paying me. I told him I did not want to do that. He slapped me and told me if I wanted to go get groceries I would sell the guy the pot.

A little later a knock came at the door. I opened it but it was not my neighbor's husband. It was a guy with long hair and jeans that looked like a hippie from the sixties. He said he was there to pick up a bag that David had sent him. He asked for my husband and I told him he was not there. He seemed put out but asked if I had a bag. Being naive and gullible, I sold him the bag.

At this time I was pregnant with our second child.

A week went by it was summer time, late summer and the ice cream truck was coming around. I remember I was outside barefoot and in shorts, standing there with my son.

We walked back into the house and there is a knock at the door. It is the police and they have a warrant for my arrest. I was scared, so very scared. They let me take my son to the neighbor and put me in the back of the police car. For my son's sake they did not handcuff me.

I sat in a holding cell waiting on my husband to come to bail me out. I found out later he had the money but he did not want to bail me out as he figured I would get off and he wanted to buy a pound of pot!!! It was my husband older friend who bailed me out and he was so upset at my husband.

I met with a detective but like an idiot would not give up my husband. It seems our house had been under surveillance for a long time by of all folks, the FBI. Luckily, it was the city that did the bust he said. He was disappointed I would not give up my husband and his friends but my husband had me believing I would get nothing.

I went to court and the judge sat there and looked at a very pregnant and scared woman. I was due to deliver by C Section the next day. He said that sad as it was, because he was pretty sure I did not even spit on the sidewalk (his words) that he had to find me guilty as to be honest I did sell the bag to an under cover cop.

He gave me three years probation and at the end of that time if I stayed out of trouble they would expunge my record.

We moved back closer to my family but things did not change. He still used drugs and wanted to even sell them. Here I had to report to a probation officer once a month and a felony on my clean record.

He left one day to go pick up drugs from his brother and party with him. His son was not even fully awake from his surgery and here he was running off. I told him if he did to not come back. I have had it and I wanted what was best for my two children.

I stayed out of trouble but this stayed on my record. Unknown to me, I had to go back to the original court that sentenced you and report in so judge could expunge it. It caused me much shame and although after sharing the whole story, it caused issues with employment and housing for me.

Years later I found out it was not expunged so I petitioned the courts and it was removed but unfortunately, though it may not show up on DOC records it showed up on city records a while longer.

Although I did not serve time I suffered the pain, fear and humiliation connected with being a criminal. I never did any thing like this before and have not since.

My advice to women who find themselves in this situation is this: No man who abuses you and uses you to sell his drugs is worth losing your freedom or your children. Get out and move on and yes I know it's hard but I did it. I went on got a degree and raised my children alone."

The reporter shares this story as though the woman spent no time behind bars; she could have and uses this story as advice and a warning you might say to other women who are in this same situation.

STORY FOUR: A CRY FOR HELP NOT HEARD (Medical Issues At A State Operated Prisons)

SUBMITTED BY: S.K.T

"My brother was sentenced to a life for a crime to this day I believe him innocent of but that is not what this is about or why I am talking to this magazine.

I want family members of inmates in prisons state and private both in Oklahoma to know they need to listen to your inmate. If she or he says they are sick and not being seen, do something. Fight for the mandated medical care they are supposed to receive and this is why.

I buried my brother this year he was only 62 not young but not old. He was housed at Lexington Correctional in Lexington, Oklahoma. He had been sentenced to life as I said but was supposed to be getting medical services.

He was diabetic and had a heart condition and received medicine for that. Then a new warden came along and she ordered all pain medication to be removed, even Neurontin, which is used for diabetics for their neuropathic pain.

For three years, he had been complaining off and on about his stomach and all they did was give him antacids or laxatives. The pain continued to get worse and I noticed in 2014 that he was losing weight drastically. They finally got a doctor that sent him off for tests. The diagnosis was stage 4 liver cancer and there was no hope.

He continued to suffer in pain and with in two months of the diagnosis was in a wheel chair. He was then removed to the infirmary and became incontinent and basically was out of it. My brother died in November 2014. The doctor that saw him in the city said he had the cancer for a while to reach this stage and that if he had been seen and screened when he first complained he could have possibly had more years with us.

My brother's last year here on earth was one of extreme pain but because he had gotten a life sentence or just because he was an inmate he was not given proper medical treatment. This was wrong ethically, morally and more. The doctor told us we had a viable lawsuit but money would not give me my brother back but this story might give help to other mothers, sisters, and children of inmates who are not seeing the medical treatment they should in Oklahoma prisons."

In all fairness to the prisons, the reporter has found that medical treatment at Joseph Harp is more than adequate and the staff there seems to care. Lexington is lacking, as are both CCA facilities, based on stories told by inmate's families and ex- staff from this facility. Medical treatment at OSP is also more than adequate. Where the reporter sees the problems are the private prisons and Lexington. Private prisons are taking medications away from inmates transferred there due to cost efficiency it seems and when an inmate needs extensive medical treatment they have the state prisons handle the case then take the inmate back.

Medical treatment is not a luxury. It is a mandated program. Medication should not be played with willy-nilly and taken away at a moment's notice. Medical staff should listen to inmate's complaints. Although some of their complaints are not real and are pain medication seeking issues, some of the medical complaints are real and serious, even life threatening. Inmates not facing life sentences are given them when medical issues that are serious are ignored.

Medical treatment, decent food, sanitary conditions, freedom from excessive unwarranted write-ups is not luxuries. They are basic and humane and need to be the rule of thumb for all prisons, whether private or state operated.

RESOURCES FOR FAMILIES OF INMATES

Unfortunately at this time, Oklahoma offers very little in the way of support and aid for families of inmates incarcerated in Oklahoma prisons, thus making the children and families a part of those some wish to forget but here are some suggestions for help:

1. Department of Human Services: If the incarcerated person is the provider for the home you must find a way to provide for yourself and your children. Food stamps, Medicaid, and even TANF (Temporary Assistance for Needy Families)
2. Local Ministers are willing to counsel with families in this time of crisis and worry.
3. ACLU of Oklahoma provides resource material, offers advice and will step in on certain cases if they deem this meets their criteria.
4. Passport to the Future is a mentoring program for children ages 4-18 who have an incarcerated parent. It is run and operated by Little Dixie CAA and serves Choctaw, McCurtain and Pushmataha Counties in Southeast Oklahoma. Other Community Actions offices may offer similar programs but this is one that was outlined on the web. Their website address is www.littledixie.org
5. As a family member do not think you do not have the right to advocate for your inmate. if you feel he or she is being abused or neglected in any form. You have to go through a lot of red tape starting with the case manager on to the Warden to the state office but speak up for staying quiet may be good at times but at other times accelerates or allows the abuse and neglect to continue.
6. If your inmate is disabled and being mistreated or is not seeing given same treatment and privileges that able-bodied inmates are contact the Oklahoma Disability Law Center. They have offices in both OKC and Tulsa and have a website with quite a bit of information.

7. Contact your local state representative and the media get the news out it may help your loved one and others

The names in this magazine have been changed to protect the inmates, the staff and the families who have stepped forward to talk to the magazine.